craft **workshop**

decorating glass

craft **workshop**

decorating glass

The art of embellishment in 25 fabulous projects

Michael Ball

photography by Peter Williams

southwater

To Angela Ball, for her faith and encouragement

THIS EDITION IS PUBLISHED BY SOUTHWATER

DISTRIBUTED IN THE UK BY
THE MANNING PARTNERSHIP
251–253 LONDON ROAD EAST
BATHEASTON, BATH BA1 7RL
TEL. 01225 852 727
FAX 01225 852 852

PUBLISHED IN THE USA BY
ANNESS PUBLISHING INC.
27 WEST 20TH STREET
SUITE 504, NEW YORK NY 10011
FAX 212 807 6813

DISTRIBUTED IN CANADA BY
GENERAL PUBLISHING
895 DON MILLS ROAD
400–402 PARK CENTRE
TORONTO, ONTARIO M3C 1W3
TEL. 416 445 3333
FAX 416 445 5991

DISTRIBUTED IN AUSTRALIA BY
SANDSTONE PUBLISHING
UNIT 1, 360 NORTON STREET,
LEICHHARDT, NEW SOUTH WALES 2040
TEL. 02 9560 7888
FAX 02 9560 7488

SOUTHWATER IS AN IMPRINT OF
ANNESS PUBLISHING LIMITED
HERMES HOUSE, 88–89 BLACKFRIARS ROAD
LONDON SE1 8HA
TEL. 020 7401 2077; FAX 020 7633 9499

© ANNESS PUBLISHING LIMITED 1997, 2002

PUBLISHER: JOANNA LORENZ
PROJECT EDITOR: JOANNA BENTLEY
DESIGNER: LILIAN LINDBLOM
PHOTOGRAPHER: PETER WILLIAMS
STYLIST: GEORGINA RHODES
ILLUSTRATORS: MADELEINE DAVID
AND VANA HAGGERTY
PRODUCTION CONTROLLER: JOANNA KING

PREVIOUSLY PUBLISHED AS *NEW CRAFTS: DECORATIVE GLASSWORK*

PICTURE CREDITS
Pages 8, 9 (top), 10, 11 and 13 (left and right), Christie's Images; page 9 (bottom), by kind permission of
the Trustees of the British Museum; page 12, The Fine Art Society, London/Bridgeman Art Library.

PUBLISHER'S NOTE
Working with glass is great fun and can fill many rewarding hours. For safety, gloves and eye protection
should be worn when cutting glass, using etching paste or working with soldering equipment.

CONTENTS

INTRODUCTION

THE BEAUTY OF GLASS HAS BEEN APPRECIATED AROUND THE WORLD FOR CENTURIES. ITS ABILITY TO REFLECT LIGHT IN SO MANY DIRECTIONS AND COLOURS DRAWS CRAFTSPEOPLE TO GLASS OVER AND OVER AGAIN. DECORATING GLASS IS RELATIVELY EASY WITH A CHOICE OF PAINTS, CONTOUR PASTES OR MORE STRUCTURAL EMBELLISHMENTS, SUCH AS WIRE OR BEADS. THIS BOOK WILL ENABLE YOU TO DECORATE GLASS PIECES BY FOLLOWING THE STEP-BY-STEP INSTRUCTIONS FOR EACH PROJECT. THE BASIC TECHNIQUES SECTION EXPLAINS THE DIFFERENT METHODS OF WORKING WITH GLASS. THE GALLERY SHOWS A RANGE OF OBJECTS DECORATED BY ARTISTS TO INSPIRE YOU TO DEVELOP YOUR OWN INDIVIDUAL DESIGN IDEAS.

Left: Among the techniques that can be used to decorate glass are painting, etching and applying wire and lead.

HISTORY OF GLASSWORK

FOR THOUSANDS OF YEARS, PEOPLE HAVE MADE USE OF THE VERSATILE QUALITIES OF GLASS, CREATING EVERYTHING FROM SIMPLE CONTAINERS TO WINDOWS AND OTHER ARCHITECTURAL FEATURES. IT IS HARD TO SAY WITH ANY ACCURACY WHERE OR WHEN GLASS WAS FIRST MADE, BUT GLASS BEADS WERE BEING CREATED IN THE MIDDLE EAST ABOUT 4000 YEARS AGO. THE SKILLS OF BEAD MANUFACTURE WERE EXTENDED TO SIMPLE CONTAINERS, WHICH WERE MADE BY WINDING SOFTENED GLASS RODS AROUND A SAND CORE, OR PRESSING DISCS OF GLASS INTO MOULDS. BY THE FIRST CENTURY BC, GLASS PRODUCTION HAD BEEN REVOLUTIONIZED BY A RADICAL NEW TECHNIQUE: GLASS-BLOWING. BY BLOWING DOWN A HOLLOW TUBE INTO A BLOB OF MOLTEN GLASS AT THE END, THE GLASS-BLOWER CAN CREATE BUBBLES OF GLASS THAT CAN THEN BE FORMED INTO JUGS, DRINKING VESSELS OR JARS BY COMBINATIONS OF REHEATING AND BLOWING.

The Egyptians and the Romans both made extensive use of glass, and the first and second centuries AD saw the flowering of glass craftsmanship. As well as ornate decorated containers of every kind, some of the earliest known stained-glass windows were being made around this time. Large pieces of flat glass were difficult and expensive to produce, and joining small pieces together in a lattice-work of wood, plaster or metal was a simple solution that resulted in elegant decorative panels.

Many of the significant advancements in glass-making and decorative techniques were made in the Middle East: cut-glass work, gilding, enamelling and glass-painting. Ground-glass work from the Middle East was traded across Europe and Asia. Glass was also produced in China and India. In Japan (where glass was held to have a special spiritual significance) glass beads were produced as early as 250 BC, and by the eighth century AD, Japanese craftsmen were producing blown glass vessels and delicate cloisonné work, in which flattened wires are used to create tiny cells that are filled with coloured glass.

Right: An unusual opaque red glass amulet of a tyet girdle or Isis knot, made during Egypt's New Kingdom, between 1550 and 1070 BC.

Left: A selection of early glass vases from the Middle East, all made in the first century AD.

By the early Middle Ages, glass skills had travelled west, and the cathedrals and churches of Europe were turned into earthly evocations of heaven with a wealth of brilliant windows depicting the saints and icons of the Christian religion. These windows, as well as being extraordinary in terms of the stained glass used in their construction, also represented a rebirth of the skills of glass-painting. Over the centuries, church windows that had been predominantly stained glass (glass in which colour is due to metallic oxides added to the molten glass) gave way to painted glass, in which the colour was applied to the surface of the glass and fired in a kiln. Most ecclesiastical glass shows evidence of both techniques in varying proportions, from early pieces where dark brown paint is used to add subtle shading to the folds of clothing and details such as the hands and face, to panels where the design is

Right: Lycurgus cup: this cage-cup is an example of the pinnacle of Roman glasswork. Small amounts of precious metals in the glass cause it to appear green in reflected light and magenta in transmitted light. It was made in the fourth century AD.

applied entirely with coloured glass paint on to a plain sheet of glass.

By the fourteenth century, Venice had developed as a major centre of glass production. Venetian craftsmen perfected the skill of engraving on glass with a diamond point. Glass craftsmen, and the chemistry and techniques of glasswork, slowly drifted through the courts of Europe, despite the death penalty imposed on Venetian workers caught disclosing the secrets of their trade. New centres of glass production developed in Germany and Eastern Europe, and in Prague the process of engraving with a wheel was revived,

aided by the English discovery that adding lead resulted in a glass with a brilliant lustre, which was softer (and therefore easier to engrave) than ordinary "white" glass.

The nineteenth century saw great developments in glass production, as technological advances made glass cheaper to produce. In the 1870s the American artists John La Farge and Louis Comfort Tiffany created exquisitely coloured and detailed windows. Tiffany also carried out extensive work on the chemistry of glass, and many of the unusual varieties available today were developed by him.

Above: A fine example of Venetian enamelling, this is a low tazza, made around 1500.

Many designers have utilized glass as a medium for decoration within architectural design. William Morris, working in the 1870s and 1880s, looked for his inspiration towards twelfth-century stained glass, and his work, like that of Tiffany in the United States, was much in demand for ecclesiastical windows.

In the second half of the nineteenth century, giant glasshouses were built to house the Great Exhibitions in France and England. These buildings represented the pinnacle of a form of design that had been developed for horticultural greenhouses; some examples still exist today, notably at Kew Gardens in London. These structures were so remarkable that many of the visitors to the Exhibitions came to see the buildings themselves.

There was another significant movement in the architectural use of glass when the designers of the Bauhaus in Weimar in the 1920s and 1930s created designs incorporating suspended glass panels. These buildings were the precursors of the glass-walled edifices that are so prominent in modern cities.

Glass is a wonderful medium for exploring colour, and several of the early twentieth-century artists made use of this potential, including the Russian painter Wassili Kandinski. He produced a number of glass paintings inspired by Russian and Bavarian folk art. The painter and illustrator Marc Chagall was also inspired to paint on glass, and he created a series of twelve glass paintings representing the twelve tribes of Israel for a synagogue in Jerusalem.

Left: "The Blessed Virgin Mary", a William Morris & Co stained-glass window, drawn for the east window of St Martin's Church, Brampton, Cumbria, England. The artist was Edward Burne-Jones.

Below: A Tiffany Jack-in-the-Pulpit vase. The Tiffany Glass & Decoration Company was founded in 1879 and became renowned for its Art Nouveau glasswork. This vase exhibits an elegant long stem inspired by the work of ancient Persian craftsmen and typical of the company's pieces.

Above: Two Venini vases, made during the 1950s and 1960s. On the left, a cigar-shaped patchwork by Fulvio Bianconi and on the right an occhi by Carlo Scarpa.

Opposite: Part of a stained-glass window designed by Philip Webb (1831-1915).

The twentieth century has seen a globalization of design, with Eastern and Western influences blending in "modern" art. Today trained craftspeople no longer have exclusive access to the necessary technology, and many people have the opportunity to try their hand at glasswork.

GALLERY

THE PROJECTS IN THIS BOOK COVER SOME OF THE MANY TECHNIQUES AND · POSSIBILITIES OF GLASSWORK, BUT WHY NOT DEVELOP IDEAS OF YOUR OWN? THE GALLERY SECTION HERE PRESENTS THE WORK OF SOME CONTEMPORARY ARTISTS AND CRAFTSPEOPLE TO INSPIRE YOU.

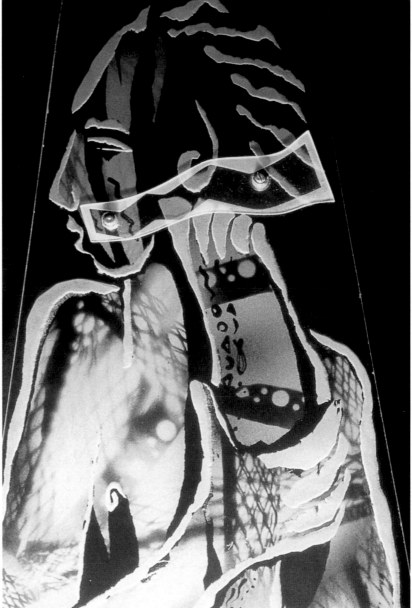

Above: CHAMPAGNE SCROLL GLASSES
An elegant design enhances beautifully shaped champagne flutes. The purple and pink background areas are painted on to the glass, then embellished with small gold motifs.
AMANDA ROBINSON

Right: FREESTANDING FIGURE
This detail is from a series of four freestanding figures, each measuring 180 x 50 cm (70 x 19 in). They illustrate a method of working spontaneously on to glass, using tape, glue, wire and twigs as resists for sandblasting. The base glass has been drilled and further pieces of coloured, etched glass attached with bolts.
CATRIN JONES

Left: FROSTED BOWLS
The gilded glass bowls are hand-painted with delicate images to produce a subtle play of light, shape and texture.
NANCY SUTCLIFF

Right: ENAMELLED BOWL
This textural bowl is created through a multi-stage process involving a double kiln firing. The first firing fuses the enamels, the second produces the slumped shape. The vibrant enamels create a base for scratched designs.
GAYNOR RINGLAND

Left: DAFFODIL VASE
A large vase made from
thick glass is hand-painted
to produce this free-style
daffodil design.
CARINA HASLAM

Above: PERFUME
BOTTLE
The dolphin design on this
small perfume bottle is
painted in bold colours,
with strong gold outlines
to enhance the curved
shape.
LE GARST

Opposite: SAY IT WITH
FLOWERS
This round glass piece,
which measures 41 cm
(16 in) in diameter, was
designed to fit a round
window. The black
outlines were painted on
to the glass first, then up
to four colours were
overlaid in each area to
create a marbled effect.
LISA ELEANOR HOWARTH

Right: STAINED-GLASS
MIRROR
Influenced by medieval
stained-glass design and
Moorish art and
architecture, this mirror
sconce is made using
traditional stained-glass
techniques.
DEIRDRE O'MALLEY

Above: MOVEMENT OF
WATER
In this panel, measuring
42 x 26 cm (16 x 10 in), a
glass appliqué technique
has been used to produce a
free interpretation of the
movement of water. The
pieces were stuck on to
one sheet of thick glass
and grouted with a flexible
filler. This method allows
the density of the black
areas to be varied to suit
the design.
PAMELA LEATHERLAND

Left: DECORATED
LIGHT BULBS
These light bulbs have
been hand-painted using
glass paints. The regular
wattage bulb casts out
colours across a room or
ceiling when switched on.
Or, if used with a plain
white lampshade, the
pattern on the bulb is
concentrated on the shade.
GRACE MILNE

Left: CLOCK
Versatile glass nuggets are used here on frosted glass as fun hour-markers for an unusual clock.
POLLY PLOUVIEZ

Above: TEA-SET
The teapot, cups and saucers are hand-painted with glass lustres and liquid gold, then kiln-fired. The spoon is made from a glass rod, using the *lampwerk* technique, which allows small amounts of glass to be blown or shaped by an oxygen jet flame.
STEPHANIE MIDDLETON

MATERIALS

M OST OF THE MATERIALS LISTED BELOW ARE READILY AVAILABLE FROM

CRAFTS OR STAINED-GLASS SUPPLIERS (SEE THE SUPPLIERS LIST AT THE BACK

OF THE BOOK). TAKE SENSIBLE PRECAUTIONS WHEN USING ETCHING PASTE, SOLDER

OR GLASS PAINTS, AND ENSURE THAT YOU WORK IN A WELL-VENTILATED AREA.

Acrylic enamels Opaque acrylic enamels are ideal for use on glass.

Air-drying glass paints are available in several varieties. Simple air-drying paints are the easiest to use, but they are designed for purely decorative use and are unsuitable for eating and drinking vessels.

Candle A heat source is useful to "flash dry" glass paint, particularly for vases, bowls and other cylindrical items. Turn the item slowly about 15 cm (6 in) above the flame, taking care not to get burnt!

Carbon paper Ordinary typewriter carbon paper will transfer designs directly on to glass (although handwriting carbon paper is better). Use a ball-point pen, as a reasonable amount of pressure is needed.

Clear varnish Clear glass-paint varnish or clear copure can be mixed with glass paints to produce lighter hues.

Cocktail sticks can be used to scratch designs into the paintwork. Cut off the point of the cocktail stick to blunt it and give a slightly broader line.

Contour paste is used to create raised lines on the surface of the glass so that colours can be applied in thick layers without flowing into each other. It can also be used to add details within a cell of colour, such as the veins on a leaf, or applied over the paint after it has dried. It is commonly available in black, lead grey, gold, silver and copper. Some suppliers also stock coloured contour pastes. Because it is vinyl-based, contour paste will also act as a mask to prevent etching paste from acting on a specific area of glass.

Copper foil is a self-adhesive copper tape available in a variety of widths. The glue is

heat-resistant, and the tape, once pressed firmly in place around the edge of a piece of glass, will remain in position while the tape is given a coating (or "tinning") of solder.

Copper wire 1 mm ($\frac{1}{32}$ in) diameter copper wire is very malleable and is ideal for beginners to wirework.

Epoxy resin adhesive is a quick-drying glue that comes in two parts and is ideal when a particularly strong bond is needed.

Etching paste Etching paste will eat into the surface of glass, leaving a matt surface. PVA wood glue, self-adhesive vinyl (PVC) and contour paste will all act as masking agents. When applied to the glass they protect the area that they cover from being etched by the paste.

Float glass 2 mm ($\frac{1}{16}$ in) and 3 mm ($\frac{1}{8}$ in) float glass is readily available from glaziers.

Flux is brushed over the copper foil before soldering to clean the metal. It also acts to lower the melting point of the solder so that it flows more easily. Safety flux is available for home use.

Kitchen paper and cotton buds are useful for cleaning brushes and wiping off mistakes.

Mirror 3 mm ($\frac{1}{8}$ in) mirror is readily available from glaziers. Transfer the shape that you wish to cut on to the mirrored surface with carbon paper.

Reusable adhesive and masking tape are useful for holding designs in place.

Self-adhesive lead can be used to simulate leaded glass. It is available in a range of different widths and is easy to use.

Self-adhesive vinyl is ideal for masking large areas of glass from etching paste.

Solder consists of a blend or alloy of

different metals. 50/50 tin-lead solder is ideal for nearly all stained-glass work.

Stained glass is available in many different varieties of colour, pattern and texture.

Stained-glass globules are available in a range of sizes, from 1cm ($\frac{1}{2}$ in) upwards.

Tinned copper wire can be soldered easily. If you find it hard to obtain, it is possible to tin wire yourself with a soldering iron.

White spirit White spirit will act as a solvent for most spirit-based glass paints.

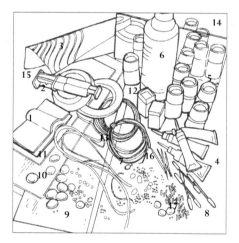

1 Reusable adhesive
2 Masking tape
3 Carbon paper
4 Contour paste
5 Air-drying glass paints
6 White spirit
7 Self-adhesive lead
8 Cotton buds
9 Stained glass
10 Stained-glass globules

11 2 mm ($\frac{1}{16}$ in) and
   3 mm ($\frac{1}{8}$ in) float
   glass
12 Copper foil
13 1 mm ($\frac{1}{32}$ in)
   diameter copper wire
14 Mirror
15 Epoxy resin adhesive
16 Cocktail sticks
17 Beads

EQUIPMENT

A WELL-LIT WORKPLACE AND A PAINTBRUSH ARE ALL THAT ARE NEEDED FOR MANY OF THE PROJECTS IN THIS BOOK, BUT IF YOU DO WISH TO EXPLORE DECORATIVE GLASSWORK FURTHER, LEARNING THE BASIC SKILLS OF GLASS-CUTTING AND SOLDERING CAN OPEN UP A WHOLE RANGE OF NEW POSSIBILITIES.

Cloth A piece of cloth or towel is useful to provide support for items such as bottles or bowls while they are being painted.

Craft knife A craft knife is useful for peeling off contour paste in glass-painting and etching projects.

Cutting oil lubricates the cutting wheel and helps to prevent small particles of glass from binding to the wheel. Pour cutting oil and surgical alcohol into a small jar until it is a quarter full, then pack the jar with absorbent material. Press the cutting wheel into the soaked material after every two or three cuts to keep it well lubricated.

Decorator's paintbrush A 3.75 cm (1½ in) paintbrush is useful for covering large background areas.

Dropper A dropper or teat pipette is useful when blending colours, as it allows you to mix paint in accurate proportions.

Fid is available from stained-glass suppliers. This is ideal for rubbing over copper foil and self-adhesive lead. Any suitably shaped wooden or plastic implement will do – such as a wooden peg.

Flux brush A small brush for applying flux when soldering.

Glass-cutter A glass-cutter is composed of a hardened metal disc or cutting wheel on the end of a handle. When you run the disc over the surface of a piece of glass, it leaves a scratch, or score, which is the line along which the glass will break when stressed.

Glass palette A piece of 4 mm (³⁄₁₆ in) toughened glass approximately 30 x 20 cm (12 x 8 in) is handy for mixing small amounts of glass paint. Most glaziers will supply the glass to your specification.

Mixing palette A plastic ice-cube tray is ideal for mixing larger quantities of glass paint.

OHP felt-tipped pens Overhead-projector pens are ideal for drawing directly on to glass. Water-based pens are easier to erase than spirit-based. They are available in black and a range of colours.

Paintbrushes Basic craft paintbrushes as used by model-makers are ideal for glass-painting. The same type of brush is suitable for applying etching paste, but it is worth labelling your etching brush and keeping it separate from any other brushes.

Permanent markers Permanent markers will write on almost anything, including glass. Available in black, gold and silver, and a range of different nib widths, these markers can be used to create designs that would take hours to achieve with a paintbrush.

Round-nosed pliers are useful for curved work. Try not to grip the wire too hard with round-nosed pliers as they will leave indentations.

Rubber gloves protect the hands when using etching paste.

Ruler for measuring, or when a straight edge is needed.

Scissors for cutting out templates or cutting lengths of self-adhesive copper foil.

Scythe stone For abrading glass edges before soldering.

Soldering iron For soldering pieces of glass together, you will need a 75-watt (or higher) soldering iron. It is worth buying a simple stand for the iron (or making one yourself from an old coat-hanger).

Sponges Small kitchen sponges are ideal for applying paint over a broad area.

Straight-nosed pliers are useful for straightening wire and bending sharp angles.

Thick straight-edge This is used for cutting straight lines on glass.

Wire-cutters A pair of good quality wire-cutters is a worthwhile investment if you intend to do a lot of wirework. However, a pair of standard electrical pliers with an inbuilt wire-cutter would be adequate.

1 Scissors	11 Rubber gloves
2 Craft knife	12 Wooden pegs
3 Gold permanent marker	13 Glass-cutter
4 Ruler	14 Cutting oil
5 Cloth	15 Soldering iron
6 Mixing palette	16 Scythe stone
7 Paintbrushes	17 Round-nosed pliers
8 3.75 cm (1½ in) decorator's paintbrush	18 Wire-cutters
9 Dropper	19 Candle
10 Sponges	20 Solder
	21 Self-adhesive vinyl

BASIC TECHNIQUES

GLASS IS AN EXTREMELY VERSATILE MATERIAL. THIS BOOK CONCENTRATES ON THE TECHNIQUES THAT CAN BE APPLIED TO GLASS AFTER IT HAS BEEN FORMED. THESE INCLUDE ETCHING, PAINTING, STAINED-GLASS CONSTRUCTION, WIREWORK AND GLASS-CUTTING. BEFORE YOU BEGIN TO TACKLE ANY OF THE PROJECTS, LOOK THROUGH THIS SECTION, WHICH ACTS AS AN INTRODUCTION TO THE BASIC SKILLS YOU WILL NEED FOR DECORATING GLASS WITH CONFIDENCE AND STYLE.

TRANSFERRING THE DESIGN

Tracing through the Glass
Stick the design in position on the back of the article you wish to transfer it to with reusable adhesive or masking tape. For curved vessels cut the design into sections. Trace the design directly on to the surface of the vessel with the tube of contour paste.

Using Carbon Paper
Place a sheet of carbon paper over the article and place the design over the carbon paper. With a ball-point pen, trace over the lines of the design, pressing fairly firmly. NB Some carbon papers will not work on glass – handwriting carbon paper is the most suitable.

Felt-tipped Pens
A water-based overhead-projection (OHP) pen is ideal for sketching free-hand on to glass. Many felt-tipped pens will also work. When you are happy with your design, apply contour paste over the lines.

Water-level Technique
To draw even lines around a vase, bowl or other circular vessel, fill with water to the height of the line. Turn the vessel slowly while tracing the waterline on to the surface of the glass with contour paste.

USING CONTOUR PASTE

Application
Before you start drawing a line with the contour paste, squeeze the tube until the paste just begins to come out, then stop. If it continues to come out when you are no longer applying pressure, gently squeeze the sides of the tube at the base. To draw a line, hold the tube at about 45° to the surface. Rest the tip of the tube on the glass and squeeze gently while moving the tube.

Correcting Mistakes
Occasionally air bubbles occur inside the tube. These can cause the paste to "explode" out of the tube. If this happens, or if you make a mistake, either wipe off the excess paste straight away with a piece of kitchen paper or wait until it has dried and use a craft knife to remove it.

GLASS-PAINTING

Using Large Brushes
Decorator's brushes can give a subtle striped effect on large background areas.

Flash Drying with Candles
It is possible to flash dry paintwork over a heat source. A candle is ideal, but take care not to burn yourself! Turn the article slowly about 15 cm (6 in) above the flame.

Free-styling
Rather than using contour paste to define individual cells of colour, apply a coat of varnish over the article and brush or drop colours into the varnish, allowing them to blend freely.

Applying with a Sponge
Pour paint on to a saucer and sponge it over the surface of the glass. Work quickly with a wiping motion to give a smooth, even covering, or dab with more than one colour to create mottled effects.

Scribing
While the paint is still tacky, scribe designs into it using cocktail sticks. Small knitting needles are also ideal. Wipe the end of the stick regularly to prevent lumps of paint from accumulating.

USING SELF-ADHESIVE LEAD

1 Peel off the backing strip and press one end of the lead into position. Use one hand to hold the end in position while you bend the lead to the shape of the design.

2 Trim the end with scissors or a craft knife.

GLASS-CUTTING

Cutting

Half fill a small jar with pieces of absorbent material such as lint. Pour on equal parts of cutting oil and surgical spirit. Press the cutter on to the oiled fabric to lubricate the cutting wheel after every two or three cuts. For accurate straight lines use a thick straight-edge or set-square. If you find that tiny pieces of glass are chipping off along the score line, it indicates that you are applying too much pressure. If you haven't tried glass-cutting before, it is worth practising on pieces of scrap glass before attempting a project.

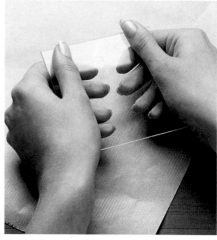

Breaking the Glass

Hold the glass with the score line uppermost and apply pressure to the glass as if you were attempting to bend both sides downwards. It is always wise to break each piece of glass immediately after scoring with the glass-cutter. Glass that is left for a few minutes after scoring is less likely to break cleanly.

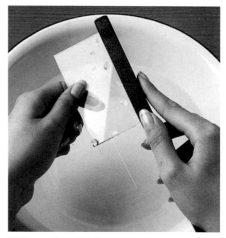

Using a Scythe Stone

Smooth the edges and remove any sharp points with a scythe stone. A little water helps to lubricate the stone.

COATING

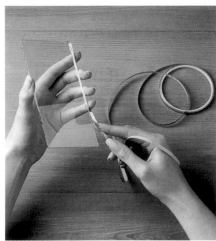

Using Copper Foil

Peel back the protective backing strip and press the copper foil along the edge of the piece of glass. Be sure to overlap the edges by about 1 cm (½ in)

Rubbing Down

Rub down with a wooden or plastic item to ensure that it is firmly fixed.

TINNING AN EDGE

Tin Edge

Melt a little solder on to the soldering iron and run it along each edge. If any edges are not properly tinned, repeat the process.

Running a Bead along an Edge

Brush flux over the copper foil and melt a bead of solder on to the iron. Move the iron along the foiled edge, adding additional solder to create a domed edge.

ETCHING

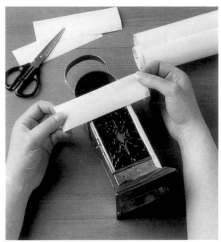

Applying a Mask

Self-adhesive vinyl and contour paste will both act as masks, preventing etching paste from working on the glass.

Brushing on Paste

Read the manufacturer's instructions. Pay attention to safety precautions such as wearing rubber gloves and safety glasses, and working in a well-ventilated area. Brush the paste on to the article and leave for the period recommended by the manufacturers.

HERB JARS

SOFT WATERMELON HUES CREATE A CHARMING BORDER ON THESE SIMPLE HERB JARS. TINY HEARTS ARE SCRATCHED INTO THE PAINT AND DEFINED WITH GOLD CONTOUR PASTE, WHICH IS APPLIED BOTH BEFORE PAINTING AND ON TOP OF THE PAINT AFTER IT HAS BEEN ALLOWED TO DRY. THE BACKGROUND OF THESE JARS HAS BEEN LEFT PLAIN, BUT IT WOULD BE EASY TO APPLY A WASH OF COLOUR OVER THEM WITH A SPONGE.

1 Using the water-level technique (see Basic Techniques), draw two gold contour lines 1 cm (½ in) apart around the top of the herb jar. With a felt-tipped pen, draw six evenly spaced dots on the lip of the jar as a guide for the heart emblems.

2 Draw gold hearts between the gold lines – one at each of the six guide marks. Leave to dry.

3 Mix the green paint with an equal amount of varnish, and the lemon yellow paint with just a few drops of varnish. Working in the space between the hearts, apply the green and yellow paint, using the brush to gently blend the colours where they meet. Turn the jar above a candle flame for a minute or so (being careful not to let the flame touch the jar or your fingers). Leave to cool.

4 Using a cocktail stick, scribe a tiny heart in the middle of the newly painted section. Repeat steps 3 and 4 for the remaining sections. Paint the centres of the gold hearts with rose pink. Draw more hearts over the design with gold contour paste. Leave to dry.

MATERIALS AND EQUIPMENT YOU WILL NEED

GOLD CONTOUR PASTE • HERB JARS • FELT-TIPPED PEN • GLASS PAINTS: GREEN, PALE YELLOW, ROSE PINK • CLEAR VARNISH • MIXING PALETTE • SMALL PAINTBRUSH • CANDLE • COCKTAIL STICK • WHITE SPIRIT (FOR CLEANING)

RIVER HANDMIRROR

THIS SIMPLE BORDER IMITATES THE EFFECT OF PAUA SHELL, ADDING AN INDIVIDUAL TOUCH TO A BASIC WOODEN HANDMIRROR. VERY DILUTE COLOURS SHOW UP BETTER THAN DEEP COLOURS ON OPAQUE ITEMS SUCH AS MIRRORS. WHEN USING DILUTE COLOURS, IT IS POSSIBLE TO CREATE OVERLAYS OF ONE COLOUR ON TOP OF ANOTHER. ALLOW THE PAINT TO JUST SET BEFORE APPLYING THE SECOND OR SUBSEQUENT LAYERS. INTERESTING EFFECTS CAN BE CREATED BY A COMBINATION OF OVERLAYING AND SCRATCHWORK AS EACH LAYER IS APPLIED, EXPOSING DIFFERENT COMBINATIONS OF COLOURS.

1 Measure your mirror, and enlarge the river handmirror template at the back of the book accordingly. It is a good idea to have a small border around the design. Cut out the design and cut a piece of carbon paper to the same size. Align the carbon paper and design on the mirror (using masking tape to hold it in place if necessary). Use a ball-point pen to trace over the design, pressing quite hard to ensure a good transference.

2 Trace over the carbon lines with black contour paste. Leave to dry.

3 Mix each paint with varnish. As the colours of the design will only be made visible by light that passes through them and is reflected back by the mirror, you will need to make your colours far lighter than you would normally, so your paint mix should contain more varnish than paint. Paint the design on to the mirror. When you have finished painting, leave to dry overnight.

MATERIALS AND EQUIPMENT YOU WILL NEED
TAPE MEASURE • HANDMIRROR • TEMPLATE • SCISSORS • CARBON PAPER • MASKING TAPE • BALL-POINT PEN • BLACK CONTOUR PASTE •
GLASS PAINTS: BLUE, TURQUOISE, VIOLET • CLEAR VARNISH • MIXING PALETTE • SMALL PAINTBRUSH

GLITTER BAUBLES

GLASS BAUBLES ARE THE CLASSIC CHRISTMAS TREE DECORATION. PLAIN ONES CAN BE BOUGHT IN A VARIETY OF COLOURS, WHICH CATCH THE LIGHT AND BRING DELICATE HUES TO YOUR ROOM. BUT FOR ADDED SPARKLE, CHOOSE SILVER AND GOLD BAUBLES AND SPRINKLE ON GLITTER TO MAKE YOUR DECORATIONS MORE EYE-CATCHING. THE GLITTER IS APPLIED BY SCATTERING IT OVER WET GLASS OUTLINER, AND YOU CAN VARY THE DESIGN BY USING THE OUTLINER ON ITS OWN IN SOME AREAS. YOUR DESIGN DEPENDS ON THE SIZE OF THE SPHERE YOU ARE DECORATING, SO HAVE A FIRM IDEA OF YOUR DESIGN BEFORE YOU START WORK.

1 Squeeze the contour paste on to the bauble. Use swirling lines or zigzags, but make the pattern quite large so that glitter will not clog up in the spaces in your design.

2 Pour glitter over the wet contour paste. You will have to work in sections, allowing each one to dry before moving round the sphere. Rest the bauble in an old glass or a roll of tape to keep it still while it dries.

3 If you want to apply glitter to only part of the piece, complete all the glitter sections you need and, when they are completely dry, add details in the contour paste only.

MATERIALS AND EQUIPMENT YOU WILL NEED
CONTOUR PASTE TO MATCH THE BAUBLES • GLASS BAUBLES • EXTRA FINE GLITTER • ROLL OF TAPE OR AN OLD GLASS, TO STAND DRYING WORK IN

NUGGET JAR

Glass nuggets have a myriad of different uses. They look effective scattered around an ornament, stacked up in a glass bowl, or even made into jewellery. Here, they are stuck randomly to the sides of a highball tumbler, making an unusual combination of colours at every turn. The tumbler is suitable for more than just drinking from — flowers look wonderful in it, or it can simply be used as a storage jar.

1 Place the glass on your work surface with supports, such as lumps of reusable adhesive, on either side to stop it rolling while you work. Mix the epoxy resin glue following the manufacturer's instructions. Put a small amount of glue on the back of each nugget, and begin to stick them, in a random scatter, on one side of the glass.

2 As you stick the nuggets on, secure each one with a small strip of masking tape to hold it in place while the glue dries – this should take about 10 minutes.

4 When the glue is dry on all the nuggets, remove the masking tape and gently wash the glass to remove any sticky traces of glue.

3 Turn the tumbler as you complete each section, sticking on nuggets until the whole glass is evenly covered.

MATERIALS AND EQUIPMENT YOU WILL NEED

Highball tumbler • Reusable adhesive • Double epoxy resin glue • Glass nuggets in assorted colours •
Masking tape • Scissors • Washing-up liquid

NIGHTLIGHTS

THESE PAINTED NIGHTLIGHT HOLDERS ILLUMINATE THEIR SURROUNDINGS WITH ENCHANTING CIRCLES OF COLOURED LIGHT. THE TRANSPARENT PAINTS HAVE ALL BEEN MIXED WITH A LITTLE OPAQUE WHITE, WHICH MAKES THE PAINT SPREAD THE LIGHT. ANY SIMPLE, STRAIGHT-SIDED GLASS WILL DO, BUT AVOID NARROW GLASSES, WHICH COULD SHATTER IN THE HEAT OF THE CANDLE FLAME. YOU COULD APPLY THE TECHNIQUE TO LAMPS OR OUTSIDE LANTERNS (BUT, IF POSSIBLE, APPLY THE PAINT ON THE INSIDE OF THE GLASS SO THAT IT IS PROTECTED FROM THE ELEMENTS).

Candle Rays

1 Transfer the template from the back of the book to the glass using a piece of carbon paper and a ball-point pen. Trace over the carbon lines on the glass with black contour paste. Leave to dry.

2 Mix the turquoise and green glass paints with an equal part of clear varnish.

3 Fill in the candle ray sections, working from the centre outwards. Mix the lemon, yellow, orange, crimson, and red-violet paints with equal parts of white paint and clear varnish. Apply yellow and lemon to each of the rays nearest to the flame, orange and yellow to the next set of rays, and red-violet and crimson to the last rays. Leave to dry.

MATERIALS AND EQUIPMENT YOU WILL NEED

CANDLE RAYS: TEMPLATE • STRAIGHT-SIDED DRINKING GLASS • CARBON PAPER • BALL-POINT PEN •
BLACK CONTOUR PASTE • GLASS PAINTS: TURQUOISE, GREEN, PALE YELLOW, YELLOW, ORANGE, CRIMSON, RED-VIOLET, WHITE •
CLEAR VARNISH • MIXING PALETTE • 2 PAINTBRUSHES • CANDLE
TWO DOVES: ALL OF THE ABOVE ITEMS AND: FELT-TIPPED PEN • KITCHEN PAPER •
ADDITIONAL GLASS PAINTS: EMERALD GREEN, LIGHT GREEN, DEEP BLUE

4 Fill in one side of the outer border with red-violet and turquoise, leave to dry or flash dry over a heat source, then repeat on the other side. Fill in the flame centre with white paint.

Two Doves

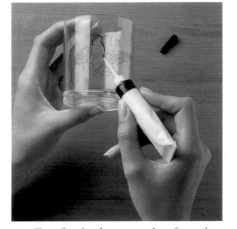

1 Transfer the doves template from the back of the book to your nightlight holder using carbon paper and a ball-point pen. Trace over the carbon lines with contour paste. Leave to dry.

2 Draw spiral branches with a felt-tipped pen (and use kitchen paper to erase any mistakes). When you are happy with the lines, go over them with contour paste. Leave to dry, then draw in and contour over the leaves.

3 Mix two parts each of crimson, orange, yellow and light green glass paints in a mixing palette with one part white paint. Paint the leaves around the centre of each spiral. Apply crimson paint to the tip of the spiral, then apply yellow to the six leaves behind that one. Blend orange into the first two leaves, then just a touch of light green into the last one. Fill in all of the spiral centres in this way, and leave to dry.

4 Mix two parts each of emerald, light green and yellow with a hint of green with one part white. Fill in the rest of the leaves, working on one section at a time. Leave to dry. ▶

5 Make sure that there are no flecks of
dust on the doves section and fill in
with white paint. Leave to dry, and fill in
the background with deep blue.

POEM VASE

THE NEXT TIME YOU GIVE FLOWERS, WHY NOT PRESENT THEM IN THIS UNUSUAL SCRATCHWORK VASE? SCRATCHWORK IS THE TECHNIQUE OF CREATING PATTERNS BY REMOVING PAINT. IT WORKS PARTICULARLY WELL WITH FREE-STYLE PAINTWORK IN WHICH THE COLOURS ARE ALLOWED TO BLEND.

INSTEAD OF LETTERING, YOU COULD TRY SCRATCHING AN IMAGE OR DECORATIVE BORDER INTO THE PAINT, OR DEFINING YOUR DESIGN USING A COMBINATION OF CONTOUR PASTE AND SCRATCHWORK. A COCKTAIL STICK IS IDEAL FOR FINE LINES, BUT WHY NOT SEE WHAT EFFECTS YOU CAN ACHIEVE WITH OTHER IMPLEMENTS?

1 The first step is to create a pair of "ribbon" lines to contain the paint. Mark two dots on the vase with a felt-tipped pen to indicate the position of these lines. Fill your vase with water to the lower mark, and carefully apply gold contour paste, following the water level. If you contour in short sections and turn the vase as you work, you will end up with an even line around your vase. Add more water and repeat for the top line. Allow to dry before you try to pour the water out.

2 Prepare your palette with the colours you wish to use, as you will have to work quickly. Apply a thin wash of clear varnish between the two lines, and brush the colours lightly into the varnish. Work quickly and apply the paint lightly to stop it from running. When you have finished painting, hold the vase over a candle and turn for a couple of minutes until the paint has dried.

3 Scratch the words of your poem, or a decorative pattern, into the paint with a cocktail stick. Clean the cocktail stick regularly with a piece of kitchen paper. Leave to dry. If the paint has flowed over the contour paste lines, clean off with a piece of kitchen paper dipped in white spirit, and apply a thin coating of gold contour paste to the ribbon lines where necessary.

MATERIALS AND EQUIPMENT YOU WILL NEED

VASE • FELT-TIPPED PEN • GOLD CONTOUR PASTE • MIXING PALETTE • GLASS PAINTS: PINK, ORANGE, YELLOW, GREEN, TURQUOISE, VIOLET •
CLEAR VARNISH • PAINTBRUSH • CANDLE • COCKTAIL STICK • KITCHEN PAPER • WHITE SPIRIT

COPPER FOIL MIRROR

COPPER AGAINST GLASS GIVES A BRIGHT, FRESH LOOK, MAKING THEM PERFECT COMPANIONS FOR THIS MIRROR. LENGTHS OF SELF-ADHESIVE COPPER FOIL CAN BE BOUGHT FROM STAINED-GLASS SUPPLIERS AND ARE VERY EASY TO APPLY. THE OAK LEAF MOTIFS ARE CUT FROM THE COPPER FOIL AND STUCK IN POSITION TO CREATE AN IMAGE OF AUTUMNAL FLOATING LEAVES. CHOOSE ANOTHER MOTIF IF YOU PREFER, BUT KEEP THE SHAPE SIMPLE FOR THE FRESH EFFECT.

1 Roll a length of 1 cm (½ in) wide straight-edged copper foil tape around the raw edge of the mirror glass, so that equal parts fall on each side.

2 Press down with a wooden peg or fid on both sides.

3 Add a second rim of 1 cm (½ in) wide straight-edged copper foil tape to the mirror surface only, covering the edge of your original border.

▶

MATERIALS AND EQUIPMENT YOU WILL NEED
SELF-ADHESIVE COPPER FOIL TAPE: 1 CM (½ IN) WIDE WITH STRAIGHT EDGE AND 1 CM (½ IN) WIDE WITH SCALLOPED EDGE •
ROUND MIRROR GLASS 3 MM (⅛ IN) OR 4 MM (³⁄₁₆ IN) THICK • WOODEN PEG OR FID • TEMPLATE • SHEET OF SELF-ADHESIVE COPPER FOIL •
SCISSORS • ADHESIVE PLATE-HOLDER DISC

Ridged Multicoloured Bottle

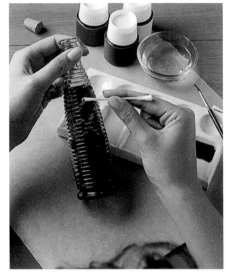

1 For the ridged bottle, paint red and green stripes across random ridges.

2 When the paint is nearly dry, dip a rag or piece of kitchen towel in white spirit and wipe off much of the paint, leaving the colour lodged deep in the recesses of the bottle.

3 Paint blocks of colour down the bottle: red at the back, yellow at the sides and green at the front. When the paint is nearly dry, dip a cotton bud in white spirit and draw three crosses down the green panel.

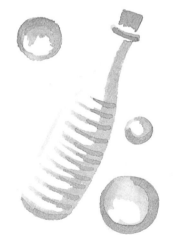

Above: These bottles can be adapted for any setting and decorated to suit their contents.

ALHAMBRA PICTURE FRAME

THIS SIMPLE PICTURE FRAME IS MADE FROM A CLIP-FRAME WITH A BORDER PAINTED DIRECTLY ON TO THE GLASS. THE DESIGN IS INSPIRED BY THE DEVOTIONAL ART AND THE REMARKABLE PATTERNS THAT ADORN THE ALHAMBRA PALACE IN GRANADA, SOUTHERN SPAIN. PERMANENT MARKER PENS, AVAILABLE IN GOLD, SILVER AND A RANGE OF RICH, DEEP COLOURS, ARE AN EASY WAY TO CREATE DESIGNS ON GLASSWARE SUCH AS THIS.

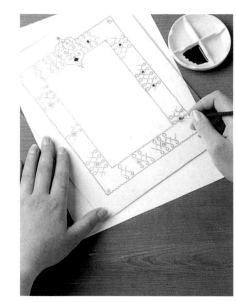

1 Enlarge the template from the back of the book to fit your clip-frame. Remove the sheet of glass from the frame and lay it over the design. Trace it on to the face of the glass with a gold permanent marker pen.

2 Turn the glass over and paint crimson glass paint over the diamonds.

3 Pour a little turquoise and a little deep blue paint on to a piece of glass. Cut a kitchen sponge into sections. Press the sponge into the paint and apply it to the glass with a light, dabbing motion. Clean up any overspill with a piece of kitchen paper and leave to dry.

MATERIALS AND EQUIPMENT YOU WILL NEED

TEMPLATE • CLIP-FRAME • GOLD PERMANENT MARKER PEN • SMALL PAINTBRUSH • GLASS PAINT: CRIMSON, TURQUOISE, DEEP BLUE • PIECE OF GLASS TO USE AS PALETTE • SCISSORS • KITCHEN SPONGE • KITCHEN PAPER

CHERRY BLOSSOM VASE

THIS VASE EVOKES THE WORK OF THE ARCHITECT AND DESIGNER CHARLES RENNIE MACKINTOSH. INSTEAD OF CONTOUR PASTE, SELF-ADHESIVE LEAD IS USED TO CREATE THE EFFECT OF LEADED GLASSWORK. AVAILABLE IN A RANGE OF WIDTHS, IT IS SIMPLY PRESSED ON TO THE SURFACE OF THE GLASS. BECAUSE THE LEAD TAPERS TOWARDS THE EDGES, IT IS NOT POSSIBLE TO CREATE THICK JEWEL-LIKE CELLS OF PAINT WITHOUT THE PAINT OVERFLOWING ONTO THE LEAD. HOWEVER, IF YOU WISH TO DO THIS, USE CONTOUR PASTE TO DEFINE THE CELLS, THEN PEEL IT OFF AND REPLACE IT WITH THE SELF-ADHESIVE LEAD AFTER THE PAINT HAS DRIED.

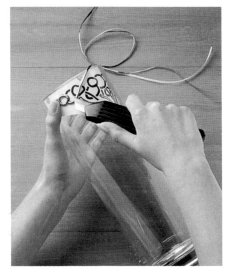

1 Enlarge the template from the back of the book to fit your vase. Stick it to the inside of the vase with reusable adhesive. Using the template as a guide, bend and stick the pieces of 3 mm (⅛ in) self-adhesive lead into position over all of the bold lines on the template. Use a pair of scissors or a strong craft knife to trim the ends.

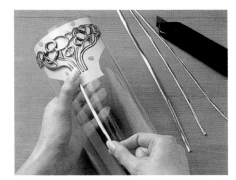

2 For the trunk lines, cut two strips of 3 mm (⅛ in) self-adhesive lead the same length as your vase, and a further two 4 mm (³⁄₁₆ in) lead strips. Press the end of each into position and down the length of the vase.

3 Splay the ends slightly at the base, and trim them so that they all end at the same point.

4 Cut a piece of 4 mm (³⁄₁₆ in) lead long enough to go around the vase with a little spare. Press it around the vase, just overlapping the edges of the trunk lines. To smooth the joins, rub over with a wooden peg or fid.

5 Mix a little white paint with matt varnish. Do the same with a little pink paint. Apply the white paint sparingly, adding just a touch of pink to each cell.

MATERIALS AND EQUIPMENT YOU WILL NEED
TEMPLATE • VASE • REUSABLE ADHESIVE • 3 MM (⅛ IN) AND 4 MM (³⁄₁₆ IN) SELF-ADHESIVE LEAD • SCISSORS OR CRAFT KNIFE • WOODEN PEG OR FID • GLASS PAINTS: WHITE, PINK • MATT VARNISH • MIXING PALETTE • SMALL PAINTBRUSH

CHRISTMAS LANTERN

PUT A LIGHT IN YOUR WINDOW AT CHRISTMAS WITH THIS SIMPLE ETCHED LANTERN. CONTOUR PASTE HAS BEEN USED AS A MASK TO DEFINE THE OUTLINE OF THE DESIGN AND PROTECT THE BACKGROUND AREAS FROM THE ETCHING PASTE. IF YOU WISH TO ETCH ON TO LARGE AREAS, PVA WOOD GLUE APPLIED WITH A BRUSH WOULD WORK EQUALLY WELL. TO REMOVE PVA, WRAP THE ITEM IN A WARM TOWEL, WHICH SHOULD HELP THE GLUE TO PEEL OFF EASILY. REMEMBER TO TAKE PROPER SAFETY PRECAUTIONS WHEN WORKING WITH ETCHING PASTE, AND ALWAYS WORK IN A WELL-VENTILATED AREA.

1 Measure the size of the glass in your lantern. Draw your own design or enlarge the template at the back of the book. Stick the design to the back of one of the glass panels with reusable adhesive and trace the design on to the glass with black contour paste.

2 Fill in all of the areas between the design with contour paste. Leave to dry. If any areas of contour paste look patchy, apply a second layer.

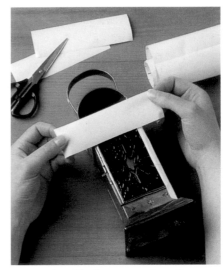

3 Apply self-adhesive vinyl to all parts of the lantern that you are not working on. ▶

MATERIALS AND EQUIPMENT YOU WILL NEED
RULER OR TAPE MEASURE • LANTERN • TEMPLATE • REUSABLE ADHESIVE • BLACK CONTOUR PASTE • SELF-ADHESIVE VINYL •
ETCHING PASTE • 1 CM (½ IN) DECORATOR'S PAINTBRUSH • CRAFT KNIFE • WASHING-UP LIQUID

4 Apply the etching paste with the paintbrush and leave for the length of time specified in the manufacturer's instructions.

5 Remove all of the etching paste with cold water. If the design is not sufficiently etched, repeat step 4.

6 Peel off the self-adhesive vinyl. Lift up a corner of the contour paste with a craft knife and peel it off to reveal the completed design. Scrub in warm soapy water to remove any residual traces of contour paste.

STORAGE JARS

LIVEN UP YOUR KITCHEN WITH THESE STORAGE JARS. THEY ARE INSPIRED BY A COMMESSO-WORK DESIGN. (COMMESSO IS THE ART OF CREATING INLAID DESIGNS WITH SEMI-PRECIOUS STONES.) THEY MAKE USE OF COLOURED CONTOUR PASTE TO ADD DEFINITION AND EMPHASIS TO THE LEMON, CHILLIES AND GARLIC.

THE BACKGROUND COLOUR CAN ALSO BE APPLIED WITH A SPONGE, WHICH ALLOWS THE PAINT TO BE APPLIED VERY THINLY WITH LITTLE DANGER OF DRIPS OR MARKS. SPONGES ARE ALSO IDEAL FOR WINDOW PANES AND ANY TIME YOU WANT TO COVER AN AREA RAPIDLY WITH A SMOOTH COAT OF COLOUR.

1 Enlarge the lemon template from the back of the book and stick it to the inside of the jar with reusable adhesive. Trace the design on to the surface with black contour paste.

2 Mix deep blue and violet glass paints with equal parts of varnish in a mixing palette. Use a cocktail stick to stir the paint to prevent bubbles forming. (Stirring paint with a brush can make it frothy.) Pour the paint into a saucer. Use a 3.75 cm (1½ in) decorator's paintbrush to apply the paint in smooth, even strokes down the jar.

3 Use a piece of kitchen paper and cotton buds dipped in white spirit to clean the background colour from the inside of the design.

▶

MATERIALS AND EQUIPMENT YOU WILL NEED
TEMPLATE • STORAGE JAR • REUSABLE ADHESIVE • CONTOUR PASTE: BLACK, YELLOW AND GOLD •
GLASS PAINTS: DEEP BLUE, VIOLET, GOLDEN YELLOW, WHITE, LEMON YELLOW (PLUS COLOURS FOR THE GARLIC/CHILLI DESIGNS) •
CLEAR VARNISH • MIXING PALETTE • COCKTAIL STICK • SAUCER • 3.75 CM (1½ IN) DECORATOR'S PAINTBRUSH •
KITCHEN PAPER • COTTON BUDS • WHITE SPIRIT • SMALL PAINTBRUSH

4 Apply yellow contour paste to the lemon design. Leave to dry.

6 Highlight the design and add delicate traceries over the jar with gold contour paste. Use the same method and different coloured paints to create the garlic and the chilli designs.

5 Brush golden yellow paint over the yellow contour paste. Mix white paint with a touch of varnish for the pith, and lemon yellow with a touch of varnish for the fruit segments.

JEWELLED GLASSES

HAVE SOME FUN JAZZING UP PLAIN WINE GLASSES TO MAKE DAZZLING DRINKING VESSELS. THESE GLASSES ARE IDEAL FOR A SPECIAL OCCASION, AND EACH DESIGN CAN BE DIFFERENT, DEPENDING ON THE BEADS AND STONES YOU HAVE. IT IS BEST NOT TO DECORATE TOO NEAR THE RIM OF THE GLASS, AS THIS CAN BE UNCOMFORTABLE TO DRINK FROM. WHEN WASHING THE FINISHED GLASSES, BE GENTLE AND DO NOT RISK USING THE DISHWASHER! THE GOLD GLASS OUTLINER HERE HAS A DUAL ROLE — IT SERVES BOTH AS DECORATION AND AS GLUE FOR HOLDING THE "JEWELS" IN PLACE.

1 Wash and dry the glasses and remove all traces of grease with methylated spirits if necessary.

2 Apply the gold contour paste in swirls to a small area only, so that you do not smudge the work by covering too much of the glass. Work in sections, adding to the piece as each section dries. Gently place the largest stones at random on to the wet contour paste.

3 Fill in the design with smaller beads — picking them up with a pin makes it easier to place the fiddly beads without having to touch the contour paste. Gently press the beads into place with the pin. Allow each section to dry before moving on to build up the complete design.

MATERIALS AND EQUIPMENT YOU WILL NEED

WINE GLASSES • METHYLATED SPIRITS • GOLD CONTOUR PASTE • GLASS STONES • ASSORTED BEADS • DRESSMAKER'S PINS

JACOB'S LADDER

THE BLUE SUMMER SKY PROVIDES THE INSPIRATION FOR THIS SERIES OF WALL-MOUNTED PICTURE FRAMES. PRESSED FOLIAGE AND FLOWERS ARE POSITIONED ON COLOURED GLASS AND CLEAR GLASS IS PLACED ON TOP. THE WIRE THAT IS WOUND ROUND EACH PAIR OF GLASS RECTANGLES IS BOTH STRUCTURAL AND DECORATIVE. OPAQUE BLUE GLASS IS PARTICULARLY EFFECTIVE WITH GREEN LEAVES, AND THE COLOUR SHOWS WELL IF HUNG ON A WALL. HOWEVER, IF HUNG IN A WINDOW, THE PLANT SHAPES WILL BE SILHOUETTED. THE POSTCARD-SIZED PIECES OF GLASS WOULD SUIT PICTURES AND PHOTOGRAPHS AS WELL.

1 Get your chosen coloured glass cut to size. Lay it on the work surface and, using tweezers, position pressed leaves on to the glass, using a small dab of instant bonding adhesive.

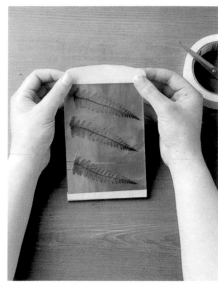

2 Place the clear glass over the leaves and apply masking tape over the edges to hold the two pieces of glass together temporarily.

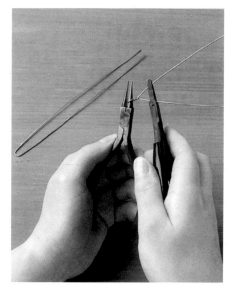

3 Cut a piece of copper wire 32 cm (12½ in) long. Gripping the middle with round-nosed pliers, bend the ends down and twist together with straight-nosed pliers. ▶

MATERIALS AND EQUIPMENT YOU WILL NEED
SIX PIECES EACH OF COLOURED GLASS AND MATCHING-SIZED CLEAR GLASS • TWEEZERS • DRIED, PRESSED FOLIAGE •
INSTANT BONDING ADHESIVE • MASKING TAPE • 1 MM (½2 IN) COPPER WIRE • RULER • ROUND-NOSED PLIERS • STRAIGHT-NOSED PLIERS

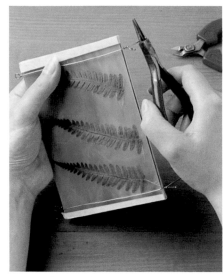

4 Bend out two ends of the wire horizontally, then make an "elbow" on both sides to fit over the edges of the glass.

6 With round-nosed pliers, bend the two ends up into loops, forming a strong split ring. Trim off the excess wire to 1.5 cm (¾ in).

8 Taking great care, lay the completed Jacob's Ladder face downwards, and make sure all of the wires are aligned. Press strips of masking tape over the wire to hold it in place.

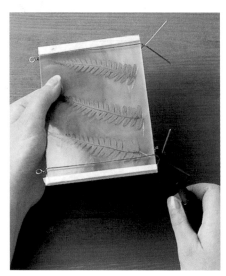

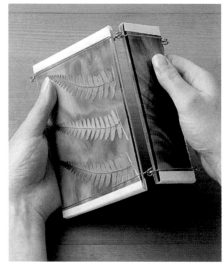

5 Position the wire around the glass and, using your fingers, bend the two ends over the edge. Use straight-nosed pliers to twist and close.

7 Cut a piece of wire 18 cm (7¼ in) long and repeat steps 3 to 6. Link the second panel by sliding the top loop into the split ring. Remove the temporary masking tape.

WINDOW TORAN

THIS TYPE OF PAINTWORK IS NOT EASY TO CONTROL, AND IT IS PRECISELY THIS FREE-FLOWING QUALITY THAT GIVES THE STYLE ITS APPEAL. SOMETIMES THE PAINT FLOWS OF ITS OWN ACCORD INTO THE MOST AMAZING PATTERNS THAT WOULD BE IMPOSSIBLE TO RECREATE ... AND SOMETIMES YOU END UP WITH A COMPLETE MESS! IF YOU DO, IT IS EASY TO WASH THE PAINT OFF WITH WHITE SPIRIT AND START AGAIN, BUT GIVE THE PAINT A CHANCE FIRST — LEAVE IT FOR A WHILE AND SEE WHAT HAPPENS. IF YOU WISH, YOU CAN EXPERIMENT AND TRY APPLYING A WASH OF VARNISH AND DROPPING SPOTS OF COLOUR INTO IT.

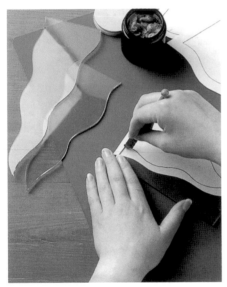

1 Enlarge the template at the back of the book to a suitable size for the window you wish to hang the pieces in. Lay a sheet of 3 mm (⅛ in) glass over the template and cut out the five sections. (Have a glazier do this if you are not confident cutting glass.)

2 Wash all of the pieces to remove any traces of cutting oil. Remove any sharp edges with a scythe stone, then press copper foil tape over all of the edges. Press down with a wooden peg or fid.

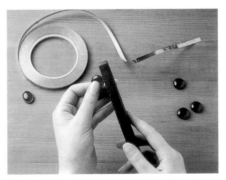

3 Using a scythe stone, lightly abrade the edge of each glass nugget. Wrap each nugget in copper foil tape.

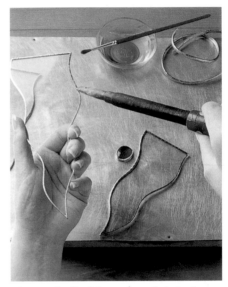

4 Brush all of the copper-foiled edges with flux. Melt a bead of solder on to your soldering iron, and run the bead along the edge of each piece of glass to "tin" it with a thin coating of solder. Repeat as necessary until all of the edges are equally coated. ▶

MATERIALS AND EQUIPMENT YOU WILL NEED

TEMPLATE • 3 MM (⅛ IN) GLASS • GLASS-CUTTER • CUTTING OIL • SCYTHE STONE • 5 MM (¼ IN) SELF-ADHESIVE COPPER FOIL TAPE •
WOODEN PEG OR FID • RED GLASS NUGGETS • FLUX • FLUX BRUSH • SOLDER • SOLDERING IRON • 1 MM (¹⁄₃₂ IN) TINNED COPPER WIRE •
ROUND-NOSED PLIERS • STRAIGHT-NOSED PLIERS • BLACK CONTOUR PASTE • MIXING PALETTE • GLASS PAINTS: BLUE, TURQUOISE, RED,
YELLOW, VIOLET, WHITE • CLEAR VARNISH • SMALL PAINTBRUSH

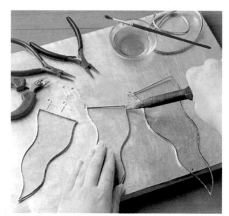

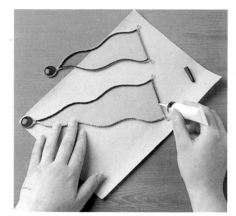

5 Cut ten pieces of tinned copper wire 5 cm (2 in) long for the hanging loops. With a pair of round-nosed pliers, grip the length of wire in the middle and bend the two ends down to form an upside-down "U" shape. With a pair of straight-nosed pliers, grip each arm of the "U" in turn and bend it upwards to form a 90° angle. Grip with a pair of round-nosed pliers while you bend the two arms downwards. Touch solder the hanging loops in place on the top of the glass sections. Wash all of the sections.

7 Apply a line of black contour paste around the edge of each piece to contain the glass paint.

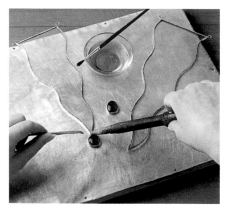

8 In a mixing palette, prepare the colours you wish to use. Mix each with equal parts of clear varnish and opaque white paint. Apply the colours thickly and freely, allowing them to blend into each other. Leave to dry for at least 24 hours.

6 Apply flux to the end of one of the sections and one of the nuggets. Melt a bead of solder on to the iron and solder the nugget in place. Melt on more solder to make it secure.

WISTERIA MIRROR

THIS DESIGN IS INSPIRED BY LOUIS COMFORT TIFFANY'S WISTERIA WINDOWS, CREATED FOR THE DINING ROOM OF HIS HOUSE ON LONG ISLAND, NEW YORK. ALTHOUGH IT IS A LARGE PROJECT IN TERMS OF SIZE, THE SKILLS INVOLVED ARE NOT COMPLICATED, AND THE MAIN REQUIREMENTS ARE COMMITMENT AND A LOT OF CLEAR VARNISH! THE SAME DESIGN COULD EASILY BE APPLIED TO A WINDOW PANE (ALTHOUGH IT WOULD BE EASIER IF YOU TOOK THE GLASS OUT OF ITS FRAME SO THAT YOU COULD LAY IT FLAT). TIFFANY IS REMEMBERED FOR HIS STAINED GLASS DESIGNS, BUT LESS WELL KNOWN FOR HIS RESEARCH INTO THE CHEMISTRY OF GLASS, WITHOUT WHICH MANY OF THE HUNDREDS OF TYPES OF STAINED GLASS MADE TODAY WOULD NOT BE AVAILABLE.

1 Enlarge the template at the back of the book to fit your mirror. Lay it over sheets of carbon paper on the mirror and tape in place. Go over the design with a ball-point pen. Go over the carbon lines with black contour paste. Leave to dry.

2 Mix light brown and dark brown glass paints with equal parts of varnish in a mixing palette. Use a cocktail stick to stir the paint to prevent bubbles from forming. Paint in the branches. If paint should happen to spill over the edge of the cell, use a cotton bud to mop it up.

3 Mix Chartreuse green and emerald green glass paints with equal parts of clear varnish. Paint the leaves.

4 Mix lavender paint with an equal part of clear varnish. Paint the flowers, adding more paint towards the bottom of each cluster. Leave to dry.

MATERIALS AND EQUIPMENT YOU WILL NEED

TEMPLATE • MIRROR • CARBON PAPER • MASKING TAPE • BALL-POINT PEN • BLACK CONTOUR PASTE • GLASS PAINTS: LIGHT BROWN, DARK BROWN, CHARTREUSE GREEN, EMERALD GREEN, LAVENDER • CLEAR VARNISH • MIXING PALETTE • MEDIUM PAINTBRUSH • COCKTAIL STICK • COTTON BUD

SPIRAL CANDLESTICK

Glass makes a great support for applied wirework techniques. The project below is a very simple introduction to wirework, but if you are more confident, why not try some more elaborate work? Thin wire can be woven around a glass support and tiny beads threaded between the wires to create tapestry-like pictures. Thicker wire requires less support and can be bent and shaped into more sculptural forms.

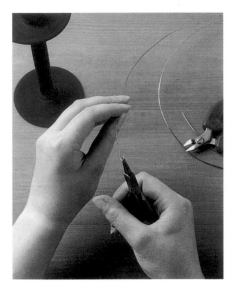

1 Grip the end of the wire with a pair of round-nosed pliers and bend a loop. Trim off the end of the wire with a pair of wire cutters.

2 Work along the wire bending gently to form a spiral. Use the template at the back of the book as a guide.

3 Bend the wire to a 45° angle, then grip the wire just below the elbow and bend to 90° so that the corner doubles back on itself slightly. ▶

Materials and Equipment You Will Need

1 mm (1/32 in) copper wire • Round-nosed pliers • Wire-cutters • Template • Glass candlestick

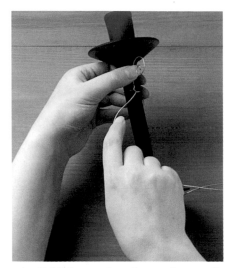

4 Hold the spiral in place at the top of the stem of the candlestick. Press the loose end of the wire around the stem and tuck it behind the spiral. Bend the loose end tightly back on itself, so that it locks the wire in place.

5 Continue to hold the spiral as you pull the remaining wire tightly down and around the stem. Trim off the end of the wire next to the stem with a pair of wire-cutters.

HEART LIGHTCATCHER

THIS PIECE OF DECORATED GLASS IS DESIGNED TO BE HUNG IN A WINDOW, ON A PIECE OF FINE RIBBON. IT CREATES BEAUTIFUL SHIMMERING PATTERNS AS IT CATCHES THE LIGHT. THE DESIGN IS TRACED DIRECTLY ON TO THE GLASS, ENABLING YOU TO REPRODUCE ANYTHING, SO YOU DO NOT HAVE TO BE GOOD AT DRAWING TO PRODUCE A PLEASING DESIGN. GENERALLY, THE LARGER THE DESIGN, THE EASIER IT WILL BE TO DEAL WITH THE CONTOUR PASTE AND PAINT. COLOURED CONTOUR PASTE CAN MAKE YOUR DECORATION A LITTLE DIFFERENT, AS CAN SCRATCHING TINY SCRIBE LINES INTO THE PAINT WHEN IT IS TACKY.

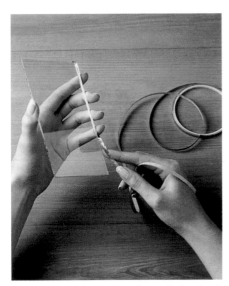

1 Enlarge the template from the back of the book and cut a piece of 2 mm (¹⁄₁₆ in) float glass to fit the design. Wash the glass and edge it with self-adhesive copper foil tape. Press down with a wooden peg or fid.

2 Bend the copper wire into two hanging loops (see step 5 of the Window Toran project for details).

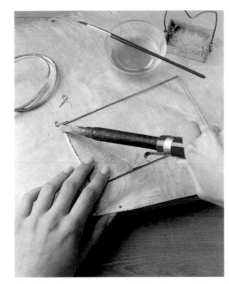

3 Brush the copper-foiled edge with flux, and then tin. Touch solder the hanging loops in place. Wash the lightcatcher. ▶

MATERIALS AND EQUIPMENT YOU WILL NEED
TEMPLATE • 2 MM (¹⁄₁₆ IN) FLOAT GLASS • GLASS-CUTTER • CUTTING OIL • THICK STRAIGHT-EDGE • SELF-ADHESIVE COPPER FOIL TAPE • WOODEN PEG OR FID • 1 MM (¹⁄₃₂ IN) TINNED COPPER WIRE • ROUND-NOSED PLIERS • WIRE-CUTTERS • STRAIGHT-NOSED PLIERS • FLUX • FLUX BRUSH • SOLDER • SOLDERING IRON • BLACK CONTOUR PASTE • GLASS PAINTS: YELLOW, GREEN, PINK, RED • PAINTBRUSH • COCKTAIL STICK

4 Lay the template on the work surface and place the lightcatcher over it. Trace the design on to the glass with black contour paste. Leave to dry.

6 Use the cocktail stick to decorate the design with scratchwork.

5 Paint the design, following the finished photograph for the colours.

Lemonade Jug

Get into the spirit of summer with this unusual lemonade jug. The same design could be applied to create a set of matching glasses or bowls. Etching is particularly suitable for eating or drinking vessels as, once the piece has been washed, there is no surface residue. On straight-sided vessels, it is possible to create simple etched designs using just a sheet of self-adhesive vinyl as a mask. Once the vinyl has been applied over the whole vessel, the design can be cut out with a craft knife and peeled off to expose the glass. The etching paste is then applied as usual.

1 Measure the top rim of your jug and enlarge the template at the back of the book to fit. Cut the design into sections and space them evenly just below the neck of the jug. Trace the design on to the surface of the glass with black contour paste. Leave to dry for 2 hours.

3 Fill in all of the gaps between the outline of the design and the vinyl with contour paste.

5 Wash off the etching paste with cold water. If the etching paste has done its job, the glass should now be evenly etched without clear patches or streaks, but if it is not quite right, reapply the etching paste.

2 Cover all of the jug (except the design area) with self-adhesive vinyl or two coats of PVA adhesive, leaving it to dry between coats.

4 Apply the etching paste following the manufacturer's instructions.

6 Carefully lift up the edge of the contour paste with a craft knife. Peel off the vinyl and contour paste. The paste will peel off more easily if you warm the jug by wrapping it in a hot towel first.

Materials and Equipment You Will Need

Glass jug • Tape measure • Template • Scissors • Reusable adhesive • Black contour paste • Self-adhesive vinyl or PVA adhesive • Etching paste • 1 cm (½ in) decorator's paintbrush • Craft knife

MEXICAN TUMBLERS

Mexican designs, with their strong colours and bold images, are extremely popular. Once you have perfected drawing chillies or cacti on paper, copy your design on to the glass with black contour paste to give a strong outline. On a smaller scale, these symbols look great on 5 cm (2 in) high glasses for a traditional Tequila Slammer. These glasses should only be cleaned with a warm, wet cloth.

1 Draw some ideas on paper first, to get used to drawing the shapes.

2 Draw the outlines of your designs on to the glass with black contour paste. Leave to dry for about 10–15 minutes.

4 When the paint is completely dry, varnish over the image areas only.

3 Colour in the image areas with bright reds and greens.

MATERIALS AND EQUIPMENT YOU WILL NEED

Paper • Pencil • Glass tumblers • Black contour paste •
Glass paints: red, green • Small paintbrush • Clear varnish

MEDIEVAL TRAY

THE DELICATE GOLDEN TRACERY ON THIS PIECE OF GLASS IS AN ATTRACTIVE COMPLEMENT TO AN UNUSUAL WOODEN TRAY. TOUGHENED GLASS HAS BEEN USED, MAKING THE TRAY NOT ONLY PLEASING TO LOOK AT, BUT ALSO FUNCTIONAL, AS THE GLASS PROTECTS IT FROM HOT CUPS AND PLATES. THE PATTERN HAS BEEN WORKED ON THE REVERSE SIDE USING A GOLD PERMANENT MARKER AND ACRYLIC PAINT OVER THE TOP. THE MEDIEVAL DESIGN WAS TAKEN FROM THE FOURTEENTH-CENTURY *LIVRE DE CHASSE* — THE BOOK OF HUNTING — AND CAN SIMPLY BE TRACED, PROVIDED YOU REMEMBER THAT THE IMAGE WILL BE REVERSED.

1 Get a glazier to cut toughened glass to fit the base of your tray. Enlarge the template from the back of the book and lay it under the glass. Secure in place with reusable adhesive and trace over the lines of the template with a gold permanent marker pen.

2 Wait for the markings to dry. With the decorator's paintbrush, paint over the gold lines with dark green acrylic paint.

3 Immediately scribe lines into the paint with the ends of two small paintbrushes held together.

4 Leave to dry, then paint over the dark green paint with light green acrylic. Leave to dry.

MATERIALS AND EQUIPMENT YOU WILL NEED

WOODEN TRAY • TOUGHENED GLASS TO FIT TRAY BASE • TEMPLATE • REUSABLE ADHESIVE • GOLD PERMANENT MARKER PEN • 3.75 CM (1½ IN) DECORATOR'S PAINTBRUSH • ACRYLIC PAINTS: DARK GREEN AND LIGHT GREEN • TWO SMALL PAINTBRUSHES

BOX OF DELIGHTS

THIS UNUSUAL BOX IS MADE FROM TRIANGLES OF IRIDIZED STAINED GLASS. FROM ONE ANGLE THE GLASS APPEARS THE SAME AS ORDINARY COLOURED STAINED GLASS, BUT FROM ANOTHER IT TAKES ON AN IRIDESCENT SHEEN OF COLOURS, AND IT LOOKS OPAQUE. ALTHOUGH THIS PROJECT INVOLVES SOME STAINED-GLASS SKILLS, THE MOST IMPORTANT REQUIREMENT IS THAT THE GLASS IS ACCURATELY CUT. MOST GLAZIERS WILL BE PREPARED TO ASSIST YOU WITH THIS.

1 Enlarge the templates from the back of the book and transfer them to the two contrasting colours of iridized stained glass, using carbon paper and a ball-point pen. Cut out the triangles yourself, using a glass-cutter and a thick straight-edge. (Have a glazier cut them for you if you feel unsure about glass-cutting.)

2 Transfer the hexagonal base shape on to the piece of mirror and cut out.

3 Smooth any rough edges on the triangles and the mirror base with a scythe stone. Remove the points on the mirror base. Wash all the pieces.

4 Apply self-adhesive copper foil tape around all of the edges of the pieces. Rub down with a wooden peg or fid to ensure that it is all pressed firmly in place.

MATERIALS AND EQUIPMENT YOU WILL NEED

TEMPLATE • BLUE AND GREEN IRIDIZED GLASS • CARBON PAPER • BALL-POINT PEN • GLASS-CUTTER • CUTTING OIL •
THICK STRAIGHT-EDGE • 3 MM (⅛ IN) MIRROR • SCYTHE STONE • SELF-ADHESIVE COPPER FOIL TAPE •
WOODEN PEG OR FID • FLUX • FLUX BRUSH • SOLDER • SOLDERING IRON • IRIDISED GLASS FOR LID • FELT-TIPPED PEN •
WIRE-CUTTERS • TINNED COPPER WIRE • ROUND-NOSED PLIERS • STRAIGHT-NOSED PLIERS

5 Brush flux over the segments and tack-solder the triangles into rectangular segments. Tack each segment to the mirror base.

7 Place the box upside-down on the reverse side of the sheet of glass you wish to use for the lid. Draw the outline of the box with a felt-tipped pen and cut out the lid.

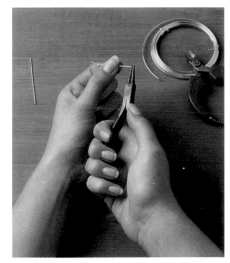

9 With a pair of wire-cutters, cut two 6 cm (2½ in) lengths of tinned copper wire. Make a loop on each end of one piece with a pair of round-nosed pliers.

6 Run a bead of solder along the joints to secure them.

8 Lightly grind off the points with a scythe stone and edge with copper foil. Heat up the soldering iron and brush flux over the copper-foiled edge. Melt a bead of solder on to the iron and run it along the edge. Reapply flux and repeat until all of the copper foil edge is tinned.

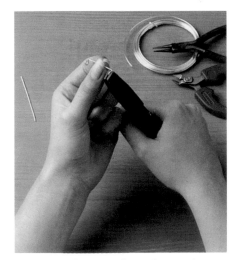

10 With a pair of straight-nosed pliers bend the loops through 90°.

▶

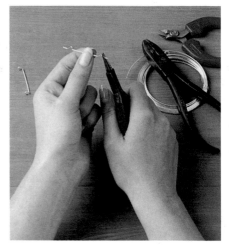

11 With the round-nosed pliers, bend two kinks in the other piece of wire to align with the loops. Trim off the ends with a pair of wire-cutters so that they are the same length.

13 Wash and assemble the lid on to the box.

12 Apply flux over the looped wire and hold it in place next to the soldered lip of the box with a pair of pliers. Melt a small amount of solder on to the iron and solder the wire in place.

CANDLE BOWL

FILLED WITH WATER AND FLOATING CANDLES, THIS BOWL BECOMES A MAGICAL ITEM. ADD SPECIAL CHARM TO A MEAL WITH SOMEONE YOU LOVE, OR FILL THE BATH AND ALLOW YOURSELF TO DRIFT INTO A RELAXING REVERIE. THE DESIGN IS BASED ON CLAUDE MONET'S "WATERLILY" PAINTINGS. MONET SPENT YEARS EXPLORING THE EFFECTS OF SUNLIGHT ON WATER, AND RECORDING HIS IMPRESSIONS IN HIS PAINTINGS. BECAUSE THE BOWL PRESENTS A LARGE BACKGROUND AREA, THE PAINT IS APPLIED USING A SPONGE. WHEN THE CONTOUR PASTE IS PEELED OFF, THIS CREATES A LIGHTNESS ABOUT THE WHOLE DESIGN.

1 Stick masking tape around the rim of the bowl. Enlarge the template from the back of the book and cut it into small sections, then attach it to the inside of the bowl with reusable adhesive. Trace over the design with black contour paste. Complete one half of the bowl, leave it to dry, then do the other half so that you do not risk smudging the work that you have already done. Draw wavy lines of contour paste across the bowl between the lily-pads to give continuity to the design. Leave to dry.

2 Mix one part each of emerald, deep blue, turquoise and yellow glass paints with one part varnish in a mixing palette. Use a brush to transfer the paint on to a piece of glass. Cut a washing-up sponge into sections, one piece for each colour. Place the bowl upside-down and sponge the turquoise and deep blue over the background and the emerald and yellow over each lily-pad. Leave to dry for one or two hours.

3 Dip a cotton bud in white spirit and clean the paint from the flowers.

4 Paint the flowers white. Use a craft knife to lift the edges of the contour paste on the lily pads and peel off, leaving the paste around the flowers intact.

MATERIALS AND EQUIPMENT YOU WILL NEED
MASKING TAPE • GLASS BOWL • TEMPLATE • SCISSORS • BLACK CONTOUR PASTE • GLASS PAINTS: EMERALD, DEEP BLUE, TURQUOISE, YELLOW, WHITE • CLEAR VARNISH • MIXING PALETTE • 2 PAINTBRUSHES • PIECE OF GLASS TO USE AS PALETTE • WASHING-UP SPONGE • COTTON BUDS • WHITE SPIRIT • SMALL PAINTBRUSH • CRAFT KNIFE

HERALDIC BOTTLE

ERALDRY HAS FIGURED HIGHLY IN STAINED AND PAINTED GLASSWORK FOR CENTURIES. MANY BARONIAL HOUSES AND CHURCHES ACROSS EUROPE FEATURE COATS OF ARMS, OFTEN WITH BLANK SPACES LEFT FOR THE ARMS OF SUBSEQUENT GENERATIONS. ANY INTERESTING BOTTLE WILL DO FOR YOUR DESIGN.

IF IT HAS NO RIDGES AROUND IT, YOU COULD USE THE WATER-LEVEL TECHNIQUE TO DRAW PARALLEL CONTOUR LINES TOP AND BOTTOM. YOU COULD ADD TO THE BOTTLE BY APPLYING GOLD OR SILVER CONTOUR PASTE TO HIGHLIGHT THE DESIGN, OR ADD YOUR OWN COAT OF ARMS OR A SYMBOL THAT IS SPECIAL TO YOU.

1 Cut a thin strip of paper and wrap it around the main body of the bottle. Mark the point where the paper overlaps itself, and cut the paper at this point. Measure the length of the strip and divide this figure by the number of sections you wish to have around your bottle. Using a ruler, mark off these equal divisions along the strip, then wrap the paper around the bottle and transfer the marks. Using a water-based OHP felt-tipped pen, draw parallel vertical lines down the bottle from each of the dividing points. Decide how tall each lozenge should be. (Traditionally they are always slightly taller than they are wide.) Draw horizontal lines around the bottle.

2 Join the points where the horizontal and vertical lines meet to create a network of diagonal gridlines. Rub out the horizontal and vertical lines with a piece of kitchen paper, leaving only the diagonal gridwork.

3 Enlarge the lozenge template from the back of the book. Cut out the individual shields and transfer them to the bottle using handwriting carbon paper. ▶

MATERIALS AND EQUIPMENT YOU WILL NEED

SCISSORS • PAPER • BOTTLE • BALL-POINT PEN • RULER • WATER-BASED OHP FELT-TIPPED PEN • KITCHEN PAPER • TEMPLATE • CARBON PAPER •
BLACK CONTOUR PASTE • CLOTH • GLASS PAINTS IN VARIOUS COLOURS • PAINTBRUSH

4 Go over the carbon lines with
black contour paste.

5 Support the bottle in a cloth to stop it
from rolling. Paint the design a few
lozenges at a time. Leave each section to
dry before proceeding to the next.

TEMPLATES

FOLK ART CABINET PP76-7

LEMONADE JUG PP74-5

STORAGE JARS PP55-7

NIGHTLIGHTS: CANDLE RAYS PP36-9

NIGHTLIGHTS: TWO DOVES PP37-9

HEART LIGHTCATCHER PP71-3

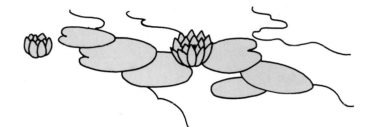

CANDLE BOWL PP86-7

ALHAMBRA PICTURE FRAME PP48-9

RIVER HANDMIRROR PP30-31

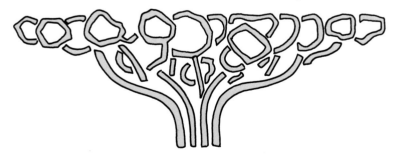

CHERRY BLOSSOM VASE PP50-51

WINDOW TORAN PP63-5

HERALDIC BOTTLE PP88-90

BOX OF DELIGHTS PP82-5

SPIRAL CANDLESTICK PP68-70

CHRISTMAS LANTERN PP52-4

MEDIEVAL TRAY PP80-81

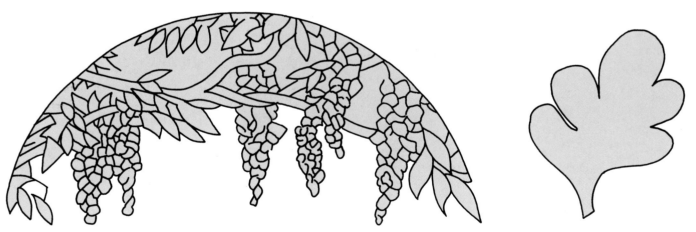

WISTERIA MIRROR PP66-7

COPPER FOIL MIRROR PP42-4

SUPPLIERS

This list covers specialist suppliers. Many of the materials are available from DIY and hardware stores.

United Kingdom
Lead and Light
35A Hartland Road
Camden
London NW1 8DB
Tel: (0171) 485 0997
Suppliers of soldering and glass-cutting equipment, etching paste, stained glass, copper foil and glass paints

North Western Lead
  Company Ltd
Newton Moor Industrial Estate
Mill Street
Hyde
Cheshire SK14 4LJ
Tel: (0161) 368 4491
Suppliers of self-adhesive lead

Codu Glassworks
43 Union Street
Maidstone
Kent ME14 1ED
Tel: (01622) 763615
Suppliers of self-adhesive lead

Kernowcraft
Freepost
Bolingey
Perranporth
Cornwall TR6 0DH
Tel: (01872) 573888
Suppliers of jeweller's round-nosed and straight-nosed pliers and fine wire-cutters

IKEA
Brent Park
2 Drury Way
North Circular Road
London NW10 0TH
Tel: (0181) 451 5566
Suppliers of mirrors and glassware

Philip & Tacey Ltd
Tel: (01264) 332171
Pébéo Vitrail glass paints and contour paste are available from selected art and craft shops — call Philip & Tacey for details of your nearest stockist

Scientific Wire Company
18 Raven Road
London E18 1HW
Tel: (0181) 505 0002
Suppliers of copper and tinned copper wire

Habitat
Tel: (0645) 334433
Suppliers of mirrors and glassware Call for details of your nearest branch

Australia
Pébéo Australia
Tel: (613) 9416 0611
Call for details of your nearest stockist

The Stained Glass Centre
221 Hale Street
Peterie Terrace
Queensland 4000

Lincraft
Tel: (03) 9875 7575
Stores in every capital city except Darwin — call for details of your nearest store

Spotlight
Tel: freecall 1800 500 021
60 stores throughout Australia

Canada
Pébéo Canada
1905 Roy Street
Sherbrooke, J1K 2X5
Quebec
Tel: (819) 829 5012
Call for details of your nearest stockist

ACKNOWLEDGEMENTS

The author and publishers would like to thank Penny Boylan for the Glitter Baubles and Jewelled Glasses projects, Polly Plouviez for the Copper Foil Mirror, Mexican Tumblers and Nugget Jar projects, Deirdre O'Malley for the Bathroom Bottles project, Debbie Siniska for the Heart Lightcatcher and Medieval Tray projects, Tanya Siniska for the Jacob's Ladder project and Victoria Salter for the Spiral Candlestick project. Debbie Siniska, Tanya Siniska and Victoria Salter can all be contacted at Glyndale, St Mary's Lane, Ticehurst, Nr Wadhurst, East Sussex, TN5 7AX. They would also like to thank: Philip & Tacey for the donation of Pébéo Vitrail glass paints and contour paste; Habitat for the donation of the bowl used in the Candle Bowl project and the jug used in the Lemonade Jug project; IKEA for donation of the mirror used in the Wisteria Mirror project; Julia Latter, Old Mill Antiques, Lamberhurst, for the use of the folk-art cabinet.

AUTHOR'S ACKNOWLEDGEMENTS
Thanks to Debbie Siniska and Victoria Salter for their dear friendship. Thank you to Jim Shalice for allowing me to use his house as a studio and to Janine Baxter for all she has taught me.
The author is pleased to consider commissions, and may be contacted at 42A Hedley Street, Maidstone, Kent, ME14 5AD, England.

INDEX